Dedicated to everyone who loves surfing and anyone who wants to live a happy and fulfilled life.

And to my supportive wife and three amazing kids who motivate me to be a better man.

surf for your success

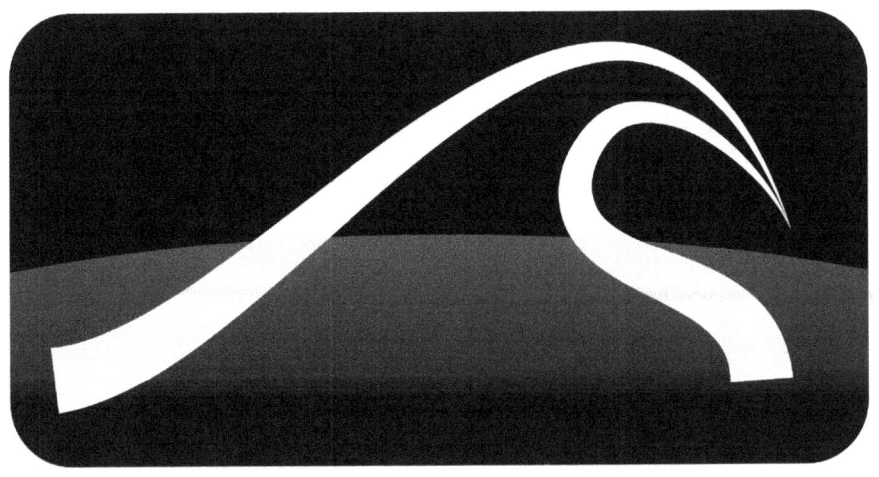

Surf for Your Success

by Brian Dawson

All contents Copyright © 2012 by Brian Dawson and SilvrStrand.com

All contents Copyright @ 2012 by Brian Dawson and SilvrStrand.com.

All rights reserved.

Published by Brian Dawson and SilvrStrand.com

No part of this publication may be reproduced, stored in a retrieval system, or transmitted in any form or by any means, electronic, mechanical, photocopying, recording, scanning, or otherwise, except as permitted under section 107 or 108 of the 1976 United States Copyright Act, without the prior written permission of the Publisher.

This book and/or ebook is presented to you for informational purposes only and is not a substitution for any professional advice. The contents herein are based upon the views and opinions of the author and all associated contributors.

Notes to the Reader:

Limit of Liability/Disclaimer of Warranty: While the author and publisher have used their best efforts in preparing this book, they make no representations or warranties with respect to the accuracy or completeness of the contents and specifically disclaim any implied warranties. The advice and strategies contained herein may not be suitable for your situation. You should consult with a professional where appropriate. The author and publisher shall not be liable for any loss of profit or any other commercial damages, including but not limited to special, incidental, consequential, or other damages.

Contents

Introduction 9

Session 1 - attitude adjustment 13

Session 2 - look up, not at your board 23

    Exercise 3.0 31

Session 4 - ask to be happy 33

    Exercise 4.0 39

Session 5 - values, personal success or destruction 43

    Exercise 5.0 49

Session 6 - daily habits 57

Session 7 - watch, be patient, then go 67

Session 8 - finding your wave 73

    Exercise 8.0 77

Session 9 - how to dream, setting yourself up for the best ride of your life   81

    Exercise 9.0 85

Session 10 - setting your goals to surf 87

    Step 1 Finding your goals 92

    Step 2 Aligning your goals 93

Session 11 - mastering the wave 99

Session 12 - dealing with wipeouts 109

Session 13 - the big wave, achieving success 117

    Exercise 13.0 121

Session 14 - fuel to feed your body 123

Session 15 - people in your life 131

Session 16 - keep moving, never stop surfing 139

About the Author 145

About SilvrStrand 148

Introduction

At every moment of our lives, we have the opportunity to surf waves both in the ocean and in life—we just need a good lesson to build the foundation required to achieve anything we want in life.

Over the years, I have helped many people start on the path toward their dreams. One thing I do not do, however, is help people achieve their dreams. This may sound odd, but I can only help people and companies start on their path and keep them motivated to achieve their goals. The rest is up to them. You may ask how this helps in life? But just like on a surf board, even as a beginner, it's up to you to stand even if someone gives you a good push. This book is to help give you that push to stand in life and surf your dreams and desires. You may be drifting without a goal or maybe you have a huge goal but have a huge challenge either way you don't have all the pieces set to enjoy the ride.

Everyone has the power to achieve their dreams—even you. The best step anyone can take for is to set goals and keep moving. As simple as that sounds, the truth is that people can work really hard and achieve part of their dreams, or work smart and achieve all of their dreams. This is why I wrote this book: to provide a set of tools and exercises which may enable you to achieve your dreams and desires. My background is about just that: helping enable others.

As for my basic philosophy, I look at challenges in life like I look at a wave: no matter what I do, I can't stop it from coming. How I position myself determines if I am going to ride, get tumbled, or miss it completely. I don't hate or fear the wave because the ride is my goal.

Life is not about you or me; it's about everyone around us. Let's get you set on the right path. It is possible to reach for huge accomplishments while living a relaxed and enjoyable life.

See you on the waves! Live happy.

surf for your success

surf for your success

Session 1 – attitude adjustment

"We must be the change we want to see."
– Mahatma Gandhi

surf for your success

Attitude is everything when you're surfing. When I hit the water, it doesn't matter what I was doing beforehand or what I'm going to do later—my body and mind simply relax. They have to, or my session will be a bust. I am focused on the enjoyment of the experience, and of course on catching waves. Throughout life I have trained myself to love a good challenge, but in reality I find all the enjoyment and happiness I need by simply being in the water, even if I don't catch any waves. When I am surfing I'm in heaven.

Ironically, I would have to consider myself super lazy, yet highly motivated. I am lazy—I admit it. I look for the easy way to be happy, but I am highly motivated to achieve my goals. The challenge I have had in the past has been remembering my happiness while achieving success. Enjoyment has come through the process of achieving.

Have you ever considered approaching every challenge the same as a wave? What would happen if you were to do so? Would you find pure enjoyment even when faced with the toughest of challenges? There are many similarities between surfing and approaching life's opportunities—life's waves—and it's possible to apply the same surfing principles toward the achievement of any goal. It takes a bit of practice to learn how to foster the necessary attitude to survive and even conquer these waves, but throughout this book I'll help you step through the process of achieving your goals—with the happy side effect of developing a better attitude!

Attitude change occurs differently for different people, but typically does so in three different time buckets (see figure 2.1). I have seen all three, but you must decide which fits you the best. The three buckets of attitude change are: immediate, short term, and constant reminder. An immediate attitude change happens for some as soon as that person learns how to make the change. A few years ago, a friend of mine, Brent, had a heart attack. Our sons are friends and played sports together. Brent was a heavy smoker, and had been smoking for many years. The doctors let him know that smoking wasn't going to help him live longer, of course, and that he needed to seriously consider stopping. For Brent, smoking was like surfing in shark-infested waters with a side of seal meat strapped to your board—sooner or later you're going to get bitten. He needed to decide: surf with the sharks or live to watch his son grow up.

Figure 2.1 Attitude Adjustment Timeline

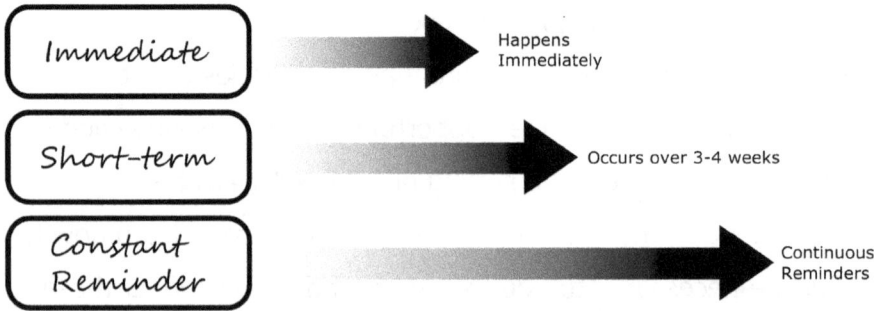

Brent is an amazing father to his son, and this experience struck a huge blow to him, like a double overhead set landing on your head. As such, he had an immediate change in attitude. The effect of that attitude change stopped him from ever picking up another cigarette. This change affected him so much that he did not even experience withdrawal symptoms. Brent's doctors and nurses kept asking if he needed a nicotine patch, but his response was "nope, I'm fine." He was out of the hospital and off heart medication in three months. And to this day, he doesn't miss smoking—he prefers instead to see his son grow up. Brent's was an immediate attitude change, he was focused on the right goal: to live and watch his son grow up. Brent's example proves that attitudes can be changed immediately with the right goals and motivations.

Not everyone has such a dramatic event to change their attitude so quickly. Sometimes changing your attitude comes with a bit of practice, over a period of a couple of weeks. The reason for the additional time could be not having the right leverage or motivation, or simply not yet having the skills needed to overcome your bad attitude. We must learn to focus on what we want to achieve: a good attitude for today. Remember, I'm pretty lazy when it comes to attitude. I want to be happy now, but I also want to be motivated to achieve my goals. I suspect you are the same. Here's an example of someone who needed to learn how to look up to achieve job satisfaction.

Several years ago I was running a team of people across four different countries. I promoted a good lead engineer named Sam to the position of manager. Sam was smart and motivated. One day I was speaking with him about his work review, and he was frustrated. Sam told me he thought everyone was against him. Wow, what a surprise! He had initially a good attitude, but now that he was a manager with a bit more responsibility, he believed he needed to always be right. He had gained a little bit of status and become one of those agro surfers who hate anyone surfing their spot.

Here's what I did over the course of three weeks to change Sam's attitude. The first week, I told him to write down everything people said or did which made him feel like they were against him. He would read each one out to me. I was again surprised when he came to me with a huge list. Each time he read a complaint, however, I found that it was a normal, everyday activity that I considered to be healthy interaction between people. It was obvious that there wasn't anyone out to get Sam— they were just trying to help. Sometimes helping meant challenging his ideas, of course, but that is different from challenging him personally. We went through each complaint, and I asked him to write down why he thought those people were being helpful.

The next week, I told him to write down what was said or done but also to write down the alternative idea of why they were being helpful. The list that week was shorter than the previous week, and he had written down all the helpful items. His attitude was already changing. The final week, I had him write down only how helpful people were being toward him—or, if they were not being helpful, how he had helped them. When we reviewed his list at the end of the final week, his attitude really had changed. He was more productive, and I had even heard a few compliments from his peers about how much they enjoyed working with this new Sam.

Sam's change occurred over a three-week period because we introduced a new way for him to process the same interactions previously considered negative. The process focused on Sam—not on the actions of other people. This is an important point: Sam changed, not anyone else. Our attitudes shape our perception of the world around us, so we should not base our attitude on someone else's actions. We cannot let the actions of others control our attitude because we need to control our own day-to-day happiness. When you're out in the water surfing, you have a great opportunity to enjoy yourself and the waves you are riding. You are responsible for paddling, popping up on the board, and enjoying the wave. If you fall, you go back out and find another wave. You don't get mad at the wave—you just position yourself for a better outcome next time.

The final bucket for attitude change involves a long and constant reminder. When we have a huge goal, one that is going to take a long time to achieve—such as a completing a college degree or learning to surf the North Shore's Pipeline—we need constant reminders and encouragement.

In early 2003 I decide to go back to school to get a master's degree. I was working full-time and my children were very young. I wanted to make sure that I could spend time with them while they were young but also that I could dedicate myself to school, work, and my relationship with my wife. For two years I slept very little, and had to work hard to maintain a good attitude. This was challenging for sure but what I realized was that to maintain a positive attitude I needed a daily reminder of why I was doing what I was doing. Just writing down what I wanted and why I wanted it helped keep my attitude positive and pushed me through the times when I was really tired.

I would love to tell you that I was perfect the entire time, but the truth is that there were times when I wanted to quit. I was able to stay at it and keep my attitude positive, however, largely because I was clear about what I wanted and why I wanted it—this clarity made the downtimes very recoverable. And this is the most important point: attitudes swing for a variety of reasons, but the ability to recover and get back up makes us great.

Every surfer falls. Falling is part of the sport, and if you don't like to fall you are going to have a bad attitude all the time. If you want to surf, you must fall. Likewise, if you want to reach a goal, you must fall and recover. Your attitude keeps you happy and what keeps you recovering from your falls. Because of a long-term positive attitude, I was able to complete my degree on time and also maintain a family. In the grind of a long goal, which is sure to have plateaus and down time, having a constant reminder to help you maintain a good attitude can be a lifesaver.

Everyone is different when it comes to attitude. What is similar, however, is that we all want to have a better attitude, or at least an attitude that fits where we want to go. If you don't want a good attitude, maybe you are someone that prefers to be mad all the time. If that's the case, you may not learn from the lessons in this book.

Session 2 – look up, not at your board

"Success is a journey not a destination."

–Ben Sweetland

When I started surfing, one of the first things I learned was to look up rather than at my board. Now I would love to say I was perfect from the start, but I had to fall a lot to figure out that my surf instructor was right. It was a warm day down in Seal Beach when I started lessons again. The last time I had stood on a board, I was eight years old in Hawaii taking lessons with my dad. Now I was an adult in my late 30s. I had accomplished much in my life, but one thing I still aspired to was the pure joy of the journey toward a goal. My instructor told me, "When you pop up on the board, don't look at your board, Brian. Look up."

That advice resonated with me, not just in surfing, but in all aspects of life. I had gone through many trainings, managements, and goals, and read hundreds of books, but all of a sudden it hit me like a wave, totally unexpected. Keep my eye on where I want to go instead of looking just in front of my feet. Once I listened to his advice, I started surfing. I wasn't good by any means, but I was standing on a board and surfing. I caught as many waves as I could that day. Surfing for me was the missing puzzle piece that brought together all the elements I had been reading and experience about all my life.

I started to apply that same surfing principle of looking up to all of my goals. Yes, I had started a great business, earned some college degrees, and had a great family, but I would have to say that though I tended to want a goal, the little bumps seemed to get me down. I'd keep trudging along, accomplishing all that I set out to accomplish, but with pure effort, not enjoyment. It was like pushing a huge rock covered with thorns up a hill without gloves. Yes, by putting my head down and pushing I got the rock there eventually, but I cut myself a bunch on the way. As I moved forward that day, however; I started to look at where I wanted to go as a guide for my own goal setting. I started looking up and enjoying the ride of pursuing the goal rather than simply looking to complete it. I do like accomplishment, but in surfing the thrill is catching the wave, not completing the ride. The end is just a fall and a good story, but the real thrill is hanging out in the water, looking for the right wave, and positioning yourself to catch it. It is the same in life: Find a goal that is worth riding, not just accomplishing. Find a goal that gives the same thrill as riding a wave because that is how you enjoy life.

When you are setting goals, there are three important points to consider:

- Session 1 - Is this something that you must do (leverage)?
- Session 2 - Is this something that you would enjoy doing (passion)?
- Session 3 - Is this something that does not conflict with who you are (values)?

Each point must align with the journey you are about to start—the ride of your life. Goals do not have to be huge (like surfing a big-wave contest) but can be simple (such as surfing the foam). Everyone has their own achievements. Goals should also not be tasks that you complete, such as taking the garbage out or waxing your board. Goals need to be achievements that drive you in your life, such as finding a new job, surfing the North Shore, getting married, having children, earning a college degree, losing 20 lbs of fat—anything worth doing, and doing well. When your goals are small, there is a fine line between goals and tasks—but I dare you to dream big. If you can't dream big then maybe you need to dream of being happy instead.

You can also look at goals like a vacation—find something that gets you excited about life and wakes you up in the morning. A couple of years ago I was setting the goals for my first company. We had a fantastic senior management team. Our VP of Finance was tasked with setting one of our efficiency goals. She was so caught up with how we were going take the goal, find the data, and measure the goal that she could not even tell me what the goal was—what we were going to achieve next year! I said, "Listen Sue, I'm not sure what you're even striving for us to achieve. When you go on vacation, do you start off before each vacation figuring out how to go on vacation, or do you figure out where you want to go?" Her response was as expected—where she wants to go. She said, "I want to go to Hawaii." My response was, "Then go to Hawaii, and take us with you." After that mental shake up, she awoke like a bear coming out of hibernation—hungry and ready to attack the task at hand. We had our goals set in a matter of days.

I'm being straight with you here—all of your goals can be exactly like going on vacation. In fact, to achieve the results you want to achieve in life, you MUST treat every goal like going on vacation. Becoming that excited about achieving the results you want to achieve has a dramatic affect on the enjoyment and outcome of your goals. When you become determined, excited, and focused, the stress melts away, and you wake up each morning alive and raring to go. Your head is up, and you are moving everything toward something that you are planning on truly enjoying. You even enjoy falling because that means you are moving toward something that you plan to achieve.

When you are surfing, you do fall a lot—in fact, to finish a great ride, you have to fall off. It is funny to think about that but every wave—even the best ones—result in you back on in the water, paddling. The enjoyment is in the ride, not the completion of the ride. The goal is the complete combination of paddling, standing, riding, and falling. Then we get back on our board, paddle back into the lineup, and wait for another wave to come again. When goal setting is approached like vacation planning, it can drive a hugely positive attitude and life changing processes. That state of being may seem too good to be true, and everyone experiences the entire gamut of feelings throughout their life, but with practice it is possible—just like learning to look up on a surfboard. There is no magic transition that occurs, just the discovery of a new perspective on something you already know how to achieve. As we get deeper into this book, we will start to ask questions that direct us to the results we want—like fuel to a bon fire with unlimited graham crackers for smores! With the right fuel, it can be that good. The fuel that you add keeps you going on the ride you choose to take.

Here comes an important question, do you even want to take the ride? I find there are four typical responses people can have when reading a book like this one. Those four types of people are:

- Yes, let's go surfing
- Yes, let's go surfing, but I think it should be done this way
- I don't believe you, surfing isn't possible for me
- I do not deserve to surf and be happy

We have people willing to try—either my way or their own way—and we have people that just won't—either because they are mired in skepticism, or because they simply do not believe they deserve to be happy. The good news is that any type of person can achieve their goal if they follow each important step.

No one can force you to ride a wave, and there is no one in the world that can create a passion in you for what you have to or choose to accomplish—the goals which you could achieve with your own internal motivation. I ask this question of you right now: Do you want to achieve any goal you set yourself up to achieve? Are you ready to look up and catch the wave or are you content with just falling all the time resulting in a happy existence? I still remember the first day I took lessons. There were people who just fell right away as if they were not willing to give a little more effort and stand up. I knew I was ready to go, but some people take a little more time.

Remember the three time buckets in the attitude adjustment. Really setting yourself up to succeed—"looking up"—comes from the motivation or attitude you put behind your goal. It's like a cheetah ready to run—you may be tired all day long, but eventually you become so hungry for your goal that the only thing left to do is run as fast as you can. Make a decision, right now, that throughout this book you will make every attempt to have a better attitude and focus on where you want to go—not where you are at. Or just make a decision to be mad all the time.

Once you have made the decision to continue, we'll apply a few simple steps to some existing goals to help you align yourself for success and remove the stress that has been holding you back. Take a moment and think back to a challenge that you faced with great stress. Now consider how you would have felt if you had treated that stressful situation with your new attitude—as if you were surfing, and the situation was simply another wave. What would have happened if you had surfed it, or just let it pass you by? Would life have been better? Maybe not in that instance, but by simply considering this, you may better understand how you want to feel.

When I started to surf and enjoy a beach lifestyle, I recognized that many of the great surfers I knew were extremely happy and relaxed, and simply flowed through life as if they were surfing. When you're out in the water, there can be a lot of waiting, falling, finding the right position—but you just can't get frustrated. After all, even with all of the crazy events happening all-around you in the world, you're in the water, probably on a warm, sunny day, hanging out and enjoying your surroundings. There's something special about being in the water, waiting for a set to arrive and soaking in the sun.

Let's apply several principles toward some of your existing goals to start to remove some stress from your life. We will get to goal setting in a future chapter, but first, let's get you to relax in the water so you can prepare for the next wave. We'll begin with the exercises below:

Exercise 3.0

1. Write down 3 things stressful in your life right now.

2. Out of the 3, circle the most stressful.

3. Write down why this situation makes you so stressful.

4. Last time you fell (or were challenged in stress) what happened? Write that out.

5. Now in that stressful situation, if you were a person just listening to the story, how could you interpret that event or situation in a positive way? Maybe what lesson could have been learned?

6. Now repeat that step for each situation. You can always use the same formula for any situation, it does work, just takes practice.

7. Repeat these steps for 4 days—if you allow yourself to be successful, you will not be disappointed.

      The attitude adjustment exercises help to position yourself for success in the following chapters. Consider this as surfing preparation where you have properly waxed your board, put on your wetsuit or rash guard, and now located a place to get into the water. Completing these steps puts you in the best position to ride some waves.

Session 4 - ask to be happy

"You'll always find an answer to the questions you ask, why not ask good questions?" −Brian Dawson

Here's a story of two people, let's call them Joe and Bob (Sorry if you're name is Joe or Bob—not meaning to hurt any feelings!).

Joe has a terrible life—at least he believes he does. In the morning, Joe's alarm goes off, and he starts complaining: *"How can I sleep in later? Can I miss the meeting I have at work to get another hour of sleep?"*

When he finally gets up, his wife and kids are up getting ready for the day. Joe starts to ask questions: "Why can't the kids get out of my way? How can I avoid my wife? She's always bothering me in the morning, asking me to do things or complaining about having too much work with the kids."

Joe gets in his car to go to work: "Why is my car so lame? I hate this piece of crap."

Joe gets to work: "How can I avoid my boss today?"

At lunch, Joe says, *"I don't want to go to the gym, how can I avoid it?"* Instead of exercise, Joe grabs a burger and takes an extra long lunch.

In the afternoon, Joe gets a call from a customer whose pretty upset. "How can I get this customer off the phone? Who can I push this customer off to? I hate this job!"

On the drive home, again Joe hates his car: *"Why can't I get a new car?"*

When he gets home, the house is a crazy place with kids running around and his wife asking for him to pick this and that up. Joe asks himself: *"How can I avoid doing anything? How can I watch the game instead of helping?"*

Finally, Joe heads to bed: *"Why am I so miserable?"*

Well, as you can imagine, Joe has been really successful today. He managed to sleep in, avoid helping out, avoid exercising, not get a new car, avoid customers, be completely useless to his family in the evening, and finally he managed to get his wish: misery. Way to go Joe. Congratulations.

Let's read Bob's story.

Bob has a great life—at least he believes he does. In the morning, Bob's alarm goes off, and he gets up: "I'm tired. How can I wake up feeling better? I've got a meeting this morning, how can I make it successful?"

When he finally gets up, his wife and kids are up getting ready for the day. Bob starts to ask questions: "How can I be with my kids for a few minutes this morning before I head out? How can I get a kiss from my wife before I leave for work? Can I do anything to be helpful?"

Bob gets in his car to get to work, "I want a new car. How do I get a new car?"

Bob gets to work: "How can I get a raise in the next annual review?" At lunch, Bob says: "I don't have much time, but how can I get a quick work out and grab lunch?"

In the afternoon, Bob gets a call from a customer whose pretty upset: "How can I calm this customer down? What do I need to do to make this customer happy?"

On the drive home, again Bob would like a new car: *"How can I save up to get a new car?"*

When he gets home, the house is a crazy place with kids running around and his wife asking for him to pick this and that up. Bob asks himself: *"How can I be helpful, spend time with my kids and watch the game?"*

Finally, Bob heads to bed: "I've got a great life. Why am I so happy?"

Again, you can imagine Bob has had a pretty successful day—just like Joe. Congratulations Bob. Now who has a better life? Bob does, of course. Both situations are alike, the difference is the questions they each ask themselves daily. No matter what you do, if you ask yourself a question you will always find an answer. Let me repeat that because it's so important:

If you ask yourself a question, you will always get an answer.

As I reflect upon my life, there were many moments in life that cause me stress from the daily challenges associated with moving toward goals. When I felt defeat, it was because I focused on the wrong things. For example I would focus on debt rather than making money or falling rather than every moment standing. I kept asking myself questions. I asked, "Why do I owe so much?", "Why can't I make money?" or "How did I get into so much debt?" I wasn't happy, and that was largely because I was asking myself the wrong questions. Once I started asking myself, "How can I save more?" or "How can I make more money?" I started making more money—and I can tell you, I was incredibly happy. Not fake, superficial happy, but the happy you get from being out in the water and catching a couple of great waves on a sunny day.

Happiness comes from focusing on the right things and asking the right questions--empowering yourself to be successful. As you progress through this book, I challenge you to ask yourself how you can use these principles in your life, or how you can find new ways of being happy. You may be one of those people who naturally asks negative questions: "I don't believe these principles work, how can I prove these principles and techniques will fail?" If you are asking these questions, again, you will find the answer you are looking for. Your result may be that you will stay exactly where you are in life, stuck in a rip tide. If you can go back to your basic attitude and make a change—if you start to ask yourself "how can I..." instead of "how can't I..."—things in your life will begin to transform. It will be as if the fog from summer has begun to burn off—it doesn't happen immediately, but soon you'll realize how great a day it has become instead of how socked in and foggy the weather is.

To start burning off the fog, focus the next exercise as if your life depends upon completing each part successfully:

Exercise 4.0

1. *Find a blank piece of paper.*

2. *Write down 3 things you hate to do and complain about every day.*

3. *For each item, write down the questions you ask yourself when you start to complain about it.*

4. *Now write down the questions you should ask yourself. Be positive. Make sure that answer can be in the real direction you want to go.*

5. *For the next three days, carry that piece of paper with you everywhere you go.*

6. *Each time you start down the negative path, read the piece of paper, and answer the positive questions. Answer them aloud if you can. Jump up and down if you have too—although may be not in a public place, unless you are that confident.*

To move toward the life you really want—a happy and relaxed life—you must position yourself for success. When you are in the water, if you are in the wrong position, you may never catch a wave—or may get pounded by waves and other surfers. The right attitude and right questions put you in a position of enjoyment and empowerment, and eliminate the stressful situations that led to your unhappiness. When the wave comes, and you are ready to ride that wave, the right questions points your board to surf down the line instead of into the breaking wave. When I think about all the tough times, if I would have been asking myself how I could be happy with a challenge, I most likely would have been relaxed and in a great mood.

When I was running my company, there was a time when my team was challenged by ever changing priorities and not enough resources. One Friday afternoon in January we were in our meeting room discussing a couple of competing priority assignments—a customer engineering project and a marketing show we needed work done on. One of our business analysts, Jake, was working through designs, getting the coding project ready for the engineering team. The engineering team came back with a huge estimate for the development of Jake's designs—to the extent that they would need to be pulled off the work they were already doing to complete the assignment. This meant our product would not be ready for the marketing show at the end of the month if we were to meet the desired timeline for the customer's project.

Needless to say, the team was a little over-excited about why none of the projects were going to get completed on time. The entire team started asking the question, "Why will the projects fail?" In a firm voice, I said, "Stop right now." I reminded everyone that we can always find the reasons we cannot do something, and I asked the inverse: "Why can we do it?" "How can we get this job done?" I brought up that Jake was an experienced engineer, so why couldn't he code the project? I started getting answers of why he can't, and again I had to remind them to just tell me why he COULD. I felt like a roadie for a rock band, trying to keep the crowd from going after the rock star. It was hard to keep order, but eventually everyone got in line. I would not take any negative answers.

As you may imagine, the meeting started to turn around and people started to come out of the fog, almost as if they were awakened from a bad dream. We could not answer all the questions during that meeting, so we decided to spend a day figuring out how we could—and how Jake could complete the assignment. We succeeding on both projects, largely because I would not allow the team to ask "why we can't," but instead to wonder "why we can."

Over the next several days, and for the rest of your life, asking yourself the right questions will lead to a better life and a more positive experience. You can decide to be a big wave surfer if you want to, and find all the reasons it is indeed possible for you to surf big waves. It is important to set expectations. If you are just starting to ask yourself empowering questions, you need to trust me here—even when it feels wrong, keep doing it. Keep training yourself to ask empowering questions. Over a period of a couple of weeks, you will start to create a habit that will empower you for the rest of your life. You've made it this far—now take a few minutes to reflect on how you can continue being successful with your goals.

As you start asking the right questions you may find time that seem as if you are trying to move forward and all you are doing is moving backward - like paddling against a rip tide. When that motion happens, it may be time to visit your values and how your values align with your goals. The values can be the key to success and happiness when you are achieving your goals. Those values can help produce answers to the questions you have just started to ask yourself.

Session 5 – values, personal success or destruction

> "If a man does not keep pace with his companions, perhaps it is because he hears a different drummer."
> –Henry David Thoreau

A winter swell is filling in at Rincon along the central coast of California, and the waves are starting to pump. The soft call of the surf has your body aching to paddle out, but you refuse to wear a wetsuit, and you don't want to be cold. Now you're pissed off because you missed the best day of the year. What happened?

Each of us has different values in life, and how those values align with your goals creates the foundation for your happiness. It's like loving surfing but not enjoying getting wet— how can someone enjoy a day out surfing if they only like being on top of their board? The reality is that you must get wet if you want to surf. Because your values and goals are not aligned, an internal conflict starts to tear at you like the slow erosion of the waves pounding against a cliff. Eventually the cliff falls into the ocean and is lost to the depths—just like your goals and happiness.

As we start to set goals, the need to align our personal values with what we want to achieve becomes the foundation for our enjoyment of the process. It is always possible to achieve success and achieve very high levels of success, but the difference is if you want to enjoy the actual entire process. Aligned values are the engine of happiness in achievement. Again, this is an important point—when your values are aligned you will be happy because everything you accomplish moves at the right speed, on right level of enjoyment, and in the right direction. This state of being becomes like the perfect wave on the perfect day, enjoyed with the right group of friends.

Values could be a new concept for you. It is important for you to understand what values are, and to know if your current values affect your happiness. I am a living testament to the trap of success without happiness. Fortunately, I was able to realign my values. Now I enjoy both.

For example, my major conflict in life was maintaining my freedom. When I redefined that value, I was finally able to start enjoying myself, and even the process of chasing my goals. For many years, I had strived for that free feeling in life, but I had never really defined it, had never sat down and thought about what it really meant to be free. I just knew I valued freedom. I had great times, but I would always set huge goals, and in reflection I realized that those goals were driven by my need to feel free.

When you set huge goals, those goals start to eat away at your freedom. For me, freedom was defined as not being controlled by others, or by external forces. When weighted down by a huge goal, I had to accomplish, I was allowing myself to be dominated by that goal. There were many times when I simply was not enjoying myself, even though I was accomplishing great things. Confusing, isn't it? Don't worry, we'll soon go through an exercise that will help you define your values. What affected me in a significant way was when I redefined "freedom." Here is what I wrote down as my definition of freedom:

> Being in control of my emotions. Contributing to others. Finding beautiful things in all people. Looking at the positive aspect of everything. Mastering and practicing skills toward my goals. Getting better and learning how to get become better.

I don't want to come across as someone who doesn't drive toward his goals—I am—but once I started living free, once I started defining freedom as something easy to attain, my enjoyment of the entire process increased significantly. This is similar to when you start really to learn how to turn a surfboard. It is a huge step toward taking your ride to the next level. Defining values helps you elevate your enjoyment of the ride. Here is a good definition of "values":

Values are the effects of the actions you take.

Examples include accomplishment, making a difference, family connection, and being controlled. There are really two types of values. The first are values that make you happy and relaxed resulting in positive emotions. While the second type of value makes you sad and upset, resulting in negative emotions. Consider it like padding with or against the current. When you are paddling with the current, your progress is fast and easy, and you get where you want to quickly and efficiently. When you paddle against the current, however...well, let's just say it's not as easy as it should be, and actually can be quite dangerous. When values are not aligned, or when they are self-defeating, it's like you are paddling against the current. You may get where you are going eventually, but it's pretty darn hard to do so, and you will end up tired.

When defining values, we want to emphasize positive values and avoid negative values. Remember when I said I like to be lazy with happiness? Try to be lazy with your values. Another important point is to never place your happiness in the control of others. Many people tend to do that when defining values. For example, if we had a value for "contributing to others", and we defined that as getting a thank you from people you helped, how often do you think we would run into conflict? I like people, but there are many folks that just aren't grateful, or may never know that you helped them with something, resulting in you not receiving your value of "contributing to others."

I can't emphasize the importance of following through with the next exercise. It's just as important as learning how to pop up on a surfboard, the fundamental move in surfing. There are other ways of surfing, of course—you can simply lie there and have a great time. If you want to stand up on a board, however; you will need to learn how to pop up. Likewise, if you want to live the life you have always dreamed, you will need to learn to stand up and define your values. The number one rule here is to be brutally honest with yourself. You do not have to share this with people if you don't want to. Just be honest with yourself—you owe it to you.

Exercise 5.0

1. Take three blank pieces of paper, and get a timer. Put a title on the top of each piece of paper: *Positive Values, Negative Values, and My New Values.*
2. Set a timer for five minutes, and when you are ready, write down as many of the Positive values as you can think of that result in you feeling positive toward yourself. Leave some space between each value. If you're having trouble thinking of values, here is a sample list: freedom, accomplishment, adventure, success, being wealthy, love, making a difference, being unique, being respected, and feeling important.
3. Go back to the first page and prioritize your top 10. Put a 1 for the most important value and proceed all the way to 10. Don't think about what you SHOULD value—instead, think about what you ACTUALLY value.
4. Under each 10 items try to define how or what you need to achieve that positive value in your life. Take your time here, be thoughtful.
5. Now pull out the second sheet of paper with Negative Values and Reset the timer for five minutes, and when you are ready, write down as many values as you can think of that make you sad, angry, or some other negative

emotion. If you're having trouble thinking of values, here is a sample list: being controlled, being disrespected, being unhealthy, failure, too much responsibility, depression, anxiety, nervousness, fear, and rejection.

6. Go back to the second page and prioritize your top 3. Put a 1 for the most important value and proceed all the way to 3. Yes I said only three, we want to think through more positive values than negative values. Don't think about what you SHOULD value—instead, think about what you ACTUALLY value.

7. Under the 3 items try to define how or what you need to achieve that negative value in your life. Take your time here, be thoughtful.

8. Now here's the hard part, really read through each of the values and determine if the value rules apply. In the next step you get to re-write those conflicting values, but for now, just put down notes where you find conflicts. Here are the rules again:
    a. Positive Values should be easy to achieve.
    b. Negative Values should be hard to achieve.
    c. Positive values cannot be dependent on someone else's actions.
    d. Values should not be conflicted, meaning that should all move you to the same direction.

9. On the third piece of paper, write down your new top 10 values. If you believe to move forward in your life, you

need new values or reorder you existing values, go for it. There's nothing to stop you, but yourself and this is your life, so you should surf the tube if you want.
10. Take a break and go get a drink, then come back to your lists.

Do you find any conflicting values? Do you find any values dependent on other people? Can you actually control each situation? Is each value easy to achieve for the positive and hard to achieve for the negative? If you didn't take a five-minute break, put the book down. Take five minutes and come back—this is important to do, as it gives you time to reflect internally. Sometimes you need to let a wave pass you by, to take a break so you can enjoy the ocean. This goes the same with some of these exercises.

Welcome back! Reread your values again. If possible, even read them aloud. Reading aloud sounds silly, but do it anyway. Now start to edit your values. Make them easy to achieve for the positive, not dependent on other people and not in conflict with other values. Just do that for the top 10 (if you have 10). For the negative values, make them really hard to achieve. You can also make these dependent on other people, but do so in a way that is really concrete. If you chose "being disrespected" as a negative goal, that goal could be defined as when someone snakes a wave from you—but that person also has to spit in your face while doing it. Now that COULD happen, and if it did, I probably would feel disrespected too. Negative values are ok to feel in the right situation—just make sure that all your values are in alignment and do not conflict with each other. Let's continue with the exercise.

11. Now take the other sheets, tear them up, and throw them away—or even burn them! Do something really dramatic. Now the old values are gone!
12. Finally, review your new lists each day for 30 days. Just look over each one, read them, and live them. If you need to make some adjustments to each value go for it and remember to keep them aligned and keep them from conflicting with each other.

There are many steps to this exercise. When you want to accomplish your goals and have passion to do so, wouldn't it be worth doing this exercise to ensure your happiness? What I've found while doing this with myself and with others is that when you really look at your values, you may find that they conflict with each other, like in the story above. As you learn, feel free to go back and change your values. As an example of change, here are Sally's values. Sally is a saleswoman who really likes to achieve results. Sally's old "Achieve Results" values are:

- She achieves results when she closes a deal with a customer
- She achieves results when her kids do their homework on time
- She achieves results when the house is clean

- She achieves results when she completes big tasks at work.

As you can see, Sally has set herself up for a perpetual bad mood because she is dependent on other people's decisions. This is important. You can only be successful in your values if you can achieve the results on your own. Your values must be dependent on you—no one else. So let's rephrase Sally's values. Sally's new "Achieve Results" values are:

- She achieves results at work when she closes a deal and gets more information to her sales prospects.
- She achieves results when she spends time with her kids.
- She achieves results when she picks up something in her house and makes it cleaner.
- She achieves results when she enjoys each day and find something wonderful to enjoy.

I always like to make sure my values get hit each day—or at least that is becomes very difficult to miss hitting my values. For the negative results, the same rules apply about ensuring that we are not dependent on other people to reach our results, except that in this case we must ensure that we phrase each so that the value becomes difficult to achieve—although not impossible. Returning to Sally, here are her old values for being "disrespected".

- When someone doesn't listen to her
- When the kids don't put away their cloths
- When someone cuts her off while she's surfing
- When people don't smile when she smiles at them

Again, with values such as those above, Sally is probably seldom happy. Sally's conflicted values make her feel disrespected every day. Sally probably complains all the time about how people were always disrespecting her, or that she feels disrespected. It doesn't matter how well her positive values are phrased—she is always feeling so disrespected that it is probably too hard for her to be happy most of the time. Plus, she has put a lot of responsibility on other people to do the right thing, and when they don't, she feels disrespected. Fortunately, Sally can rephrase her values and get back on track. We need to remember that it's ok to feel disrespected. If you really are disrespected, negative feelings naturally occur.

Sally's new "disrespected" values:

- When someone throws seaweed at her after they cut her off on a surfboard.
- When someone spits on her on purpose.

Notice that we have made these negative values pretty difficult to manifest. If they do occur, well, Sally should feel disrespected. The point here, however, is to make the "against the current" values really hard to achieve.

Now go back to your values and spend 15 minutes or more making sure all your values are all in alignment. Think of them as waves in a blue corduroy set, all moving at the same speed and creating a perfect break. When your values are healthy, many things fall into place in life and happiness.

We've created a perfect base from which to progress toward setting our goals. I am proud of you for having allowed yourself to accomplish each exercise, and for spending time investing in yourself. If you can't surf the small soft waves, then you are not going to be successful with larger waves. Once you have your values aligned, be prepared to experience a high level of happiness. Each step we take on these chapters help to align you to the goals you really want to accomplish in life. The transformation each day prepares you to emotionally and mentally align yourself to achievement.

Session 6 - daily habits

"Destiny is not a matter of chance, it is a matter of choice. It is not something to be waited for, but rather something to be achieved." -Williams Jennings Bryan.

When anyone decides to surf for the first time, they don't just paddle straight out into big surf. Usually, if you are smart, you learn to pop up on the board while it is still on the beach. Then, after days, weeks, and even months of learning, practicing, and understanding waves, breaking patterns, and how to suffer through getting hit by a huge wave and forced to the bottom like a forgotten sock in the washing machine, you find the perfect beach and the perfect wave, and paddle out...only to have the wave tell you to get lost by breaking your favorite surfboard. Yet you don't give up. You go buy another board and spend more time in the water, finally getting your chance to ride...when you suddenly fall sick. After years of these setbacks, you finally get a chance and succeed. The ride is crazy and fun, but the entire journey is your story, and you wrote it. In life, each goal is different, with its own unique set of challenges, but the same attitude and persistence which led you to success on a surfboard can lead you to success in anything, from getting a new job to simply being happy.

When I was 17 and playing high school football, my coach made me continuously practice blocking. I was the small offensive guard—basically I was slow and strong—but I had a lot of heart and drive to help my teammates. When the offensive line all stood side-by-side, I was the valley in the middle—it was pretty obvious. Over and over, my coach would drill into me the right stance and launch path. I can still remember getting in the position, listening to the count, and firing off the line to set up my block. Twenty years later, I probably can still do that same move in my sleep. I am not sure how successful I would be but I think I'd look good for the first second or two before getting sent back in time. All that practice paid off—I was named on the league squad even as a small sized lineman.

Everyone has a story where practice made perfect—from surfers to sunbathers to chefs and artists. Practicing is just a daily habit you do to gain what you want out of life. If you want to achieve some goal, you need to accept that you will get better only with practice. This applies to enjoyment, relationships, being happy, being wealthy, being healthy, and more. The first time I heard that I would need to practice being happy was from a coach for a public speaking class I was learning to teach. He told me that if I want to smile, I should just do it—even if I don't feel like smiling. I had to smile to myself. Eventually, I got it. It took a while, but I figured it out. When I practiced enjoying myself and being happy, I didn't necessarily feel happy all the time. But over time, just like in any sport, it became the core of what and who I am. I am happy because I took the time to practice, even when times were not necessarily enjoyable.

Consider how much time you spend each day thinking about all the bad things in your life, or all the things you want but do not have. Maybe you have even figured out how to be depressed all the time. What if you were to flip that and spend the same amount of time trying to be a better person, or thinking of all the great things that have happened in your life? You would feel energized, grateful, and happy, and probably experience way more success in life. When I go out surfing, I completely forget about everything bad going on in my life. Just the act of getting in the water relaxes me and helps me to have a good time. Every wave I catch, I try to improve. Every wave is really a practice session for surfing.

Maybe, like me, you have been told more times that you must practice if you want to get good. The funny thing is people don't seem to want to practice to have a happier life. If you have ever been good at something, you know the time practicing required to develop that level of proficiency. But once we accomplish something, we feel great—like we can climb a huge mountain or ride any wave. You're not a kook anymore, but an honest to goodness surfer.

To achieve success in the pursuit of any goal you must take steps, repeating them until you can do them automatically. Repetition and a positive attitude help you develop mastery of any skill. My point is that there are steps to everything in life, and the same applies to your attitude and any changes that you want to manifest. As in surfing, if you want to master life, there are activities you need to do every day. Daily habits create an attitude habit factory. The results are astonishing. Not only can a concerted effort at developing good habits make you a better surfer, but also it can also create a better attitude, or even relationship.

To learn to be relaxed and happy every day, you must establish the right habits and achieve a surfer state of mind—pure enjoyment of riding life's waves. Quick warning: It's not as easy as it looks to develop a habit. To do so, you have to go through four stages. But you can control the time of each stage. Technically they are called unconscious incompetence, conscious incompetence, conscious competence, and unconscious competence. To keep it simple, let's use the following metaphors:

1. Lame ass kook—you don't even know what you're doing wrong, or why you are considered a kook. Basically you're falling and cutting people off. You're not even sure where to start.
2. Self-admitted kook—Well, at least you recognize what you're doing wrong, but you're still a kook. You probably try to surf but are often heard admitting to others that you are learning and are eager to take in the lessons given to you.
3. Amateur—You're having fun. Still falling, but having fun, and playing by the ocean's rules.
4. Pro—You're ripping up the waves and respecting the ocean and the people surfing it. You don't even think about what you are doing, you just do it.

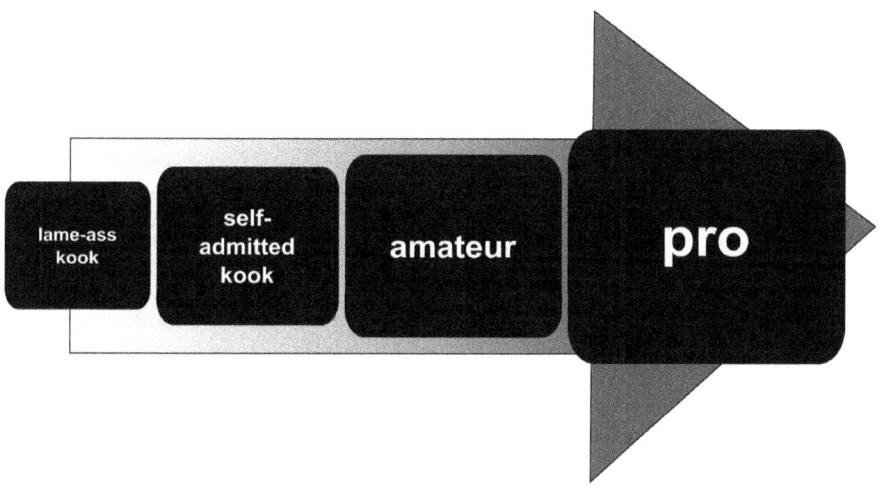

Daily habits starts us on the path toward being a pro. They give you the tools to get better and push yourself beyond the kook stage. It's important to establish simple steps toward success, and then to increase the challenge once you've achieved pro status.

Let me give you an example. When I started down the path of goal setting, I got easily discouraged—largely because I had huge goals. It was easy for me to imagine achieving those goals, but sometimes the steps necessary to achieve them were mind-boggling. So I adopted a simple habit. Each morning when I got up I would open my laptop and read through each of my goals for the year. These goals could be a simple as loving my kids more or making $10,000 this month. First I would imagine I had achieved that goal and would experience how it felt to do so. Then I would write out a question and answer it.

Question: **What is one thing I will do to earn $1,000 today?**

Answer: **I will make five sales calls to my clients.**

For surfing:

Question: How will I become a better surfer today?

Answer: When I go out, I will watch the waves and other surfers for five minutes before paddling out.

Another example of a daily habit is to exercise, or to eat something healthy for lunch instead of a double bacon burger. Of course, your daily habits may need to be aligned with your goals. We're going to work together to set your goals later in the book, but for now you should start with a couple of simple attitude changing habits.

Exercise 6.0

Step 1: Go back to the chapter where you wrote down a couple of empowering questions. Also look at the top three values you want to feel as a result each day.

Step 2: On a piece of paper, write down your top goal.

Step 3: Under that goal, write down how your life would be better if you were able to get this results every day.

Step 4: Write down your empowering question. "What do I have to do today to achieve my <insert value> today?"

Step 5: Write the answer down.

Step 6: Take about one minute to feel like you really accomplished that step.

Step 7: Repeat steps 2-6 for top value two and three.

Step 8: Repeat this exercise daily for 30 days.

Again, just like when surfing for the first time, it is possible that you will feel wobbly, tipsy, and as if you are going to fall. You may not even know how to get on your board. But just like surfing, the feeling of accomplishment is so great that you just keep on doing it. If you want to feel great, do the daily exercise. If you do not want to feel good, then don't do the exercise. It's pretty simple.

Remember the old movie "Karate Kid?" The young aspirant washed cars and painted fences. In the new version of the movie, he puts on, takes off, and hangs a coat up. What happens in the end? He wins his tournament. If you want to win, sometimes you have to establish a daily set of habits—and believe that they will work. My first day of surfing, I had to lie on my stomach and pop up way too many times, or so I thought, before we headed for the waves. The purpose was to train my body to do the right moves before I needed them.

As you progress through this book, make sure to continue with your daily habits. You may change those habits once we're re-arranged your goals, but it's the foundation you need to start establishing right now. As with any great change, you've got to be a little bit patient. Don't worry though—you're a surfer, and surfers tend to be patient. We're always waiting for a set to arrive. Now take that patience to life's waves.

Session 7 – watch, be patient, then go

"Nothing great has ever been achieved without enthusiasm." –Ralph Waldo Emerson

One thing I first noticed when I started surfing was the patience of some surfers—especially the really good ones. They didn't just run out into the waves, they waited patiently, watching either the break or distant waves coming like a circus psychic gazing into a magic crystal ball, predicting when the waves would come. Once I started to become more patient, I started noticing waves that seemed to come from far off, and to move myself into position to catch those waves. I relaxed and allowed the events around me to occur on their own time as I positioned myself to catch the wave I wanted—not the others that came and went. Imagine in life if you knew for certain your goals were going to be achieved—that you would be in the right position at the right time. How would you live differently?

Patience is something that takes time to develop, in all situations. It takes time to allow ourselves to accept that what we want is not just around the corner but may be days, weeks, months, or even years in the future. Take something as simple as a job interview as an example.

I have done a lot of job interviews over my career, and I can always recognize experience and true confidence in someone, even in the first few minutes of an interview. Interestingly, I recognize it by the questions the person asks me, not by the questions I ask them. When someone is sitting across from me and immediately starts to tell me how great they are or what they have accomplished, without even knowing what I am looking for in a new employee, this indicates to me that they are trying to prove to me how great they are versus how well they would fit the job opening. This is like a surfer running out into the waves without even seeing where the break is, or what the conditions are like—running blind, in essence. In both the interview and the surfing example, if that person were to take a moment to assess the situation and determine the relevant steps necessary, they would be in a better position to ride the wave. Setting goals is the same—it is important to take a moment and consider what you really want, and why, before positioning yourself to achieve your goal.

Consider the situation in which your partner comes home and has had a horrible day. Now, if you are relaxed and patient in allowing the wave to come, you may discern if your partner is upset with you, or just upset in general. Maybe they come how and start grumbling, getting sharp with you, or seriously complaining about nothing. You can react in two ways: You can push back right away because your partner just ruined your good mood, or you can wait and listen. What would happen if you looked at the situation like a new surf spot? Just watch for a minute, observe and listen. Then ask questions that acknowledge the behavior without accepting it. For example: "Wow, seems like something happened today. What do you need to make it better?" In this example, I acknowledged something happened, and used my empowering questions to determine how to make it better. I didn't rush to a conclusion. I took time to allow the situation to develop. Remember, don't get mad at the wave—just learn how to position yourself to either ride it or let it pass.

The toughest challenge for many people is being patient. However, this also can be the most fun part of life—being patient and working toward achieving your goals. Especially, when it is concerning life and changing your own attitude, it is important that you put in the time to receive what you want out of life. If you want to ride the biggest wave in the world, you don't just go out your back door, jump in the water, and start paddling. You have to train, practice, and set up a crew to drag your ass out of the water if you fall, watch the weather patterns, and find the perfect break. You may have to wait years—seriously! If you want to do it, you can. Often you aren't even thinking about patience—you're anticipating the arrival of the wave. Do you know why you're excited about it? Because you know it will come. Nature produces storms, and if you want to ride a huge wave, you can't change nature—but you can observe it so that you can be in the right position at the right time to hit the wave. This still doesn't guarantee anything, but at least you're in the best possible position to surf a massive mountain of water.

Taking time to watch, learn, and position yourself for success removes stress and worry and allows you to enjoy the entire process. As you become patient—and most importantly, observant—you notice things many people miss completely. You may also find your own wave, or niche in life that you never really noticed before. As you move into the goal-setting process, remember to be patient and set the right goals for yourself—and take the time to complete each step and daily exercises. I, for one, often tend to rush, but when I am patient and take my time, things always work out better and I always enjoy the process more than when I am rushing and falling. As we work through your goals, it is important for you to set goals which you really want to achieve, and that will produce clear results.

Part of setting the right goals is determining what you really want out of life. Wanting huge goals is ok, but wanting small goals is also ok. Nobody should control your dreams but you, and going after a dream should be fun, just like surfing a wave—the ride is so good that it makes you want another and another!

Session 8 – finding your wave

"Go confidently in the direction of your dreams. Live the life you have imagined." –Henry David Thoreau

surf for your success

Are you one of those surfers that spends two hours finding the right break or are you simply satisfied with the break you always surf? Each surfer is different, and each wave is different for each person. That makes surfing fun—you must respect the wave, thank the ocean, and enjoy the ride. And you're always looking for your perfect wave.

Everyone I know has a different surf style. Some people like longboards, while others like shortboards. Great surfboard shapers fit the board to the style of the person. Can you imagine trying to surf a piece of plywood? Some people may like it. When we look for what we are good at, and we find it, maybe it's time to focus on achieving what we desire and good at. I have changed focus a few times in my life, and each time I went through a learning phase. Life is full of opportunities, and finding your niche or your wave is an important step in life. Think through a time when you simply enjoyed everything you were accomplishing. Even if it were the most mundane of tasks, you enjoyed completing it. Now think about a time when you hated what you were doing—or may be a time when you were surfing in a place where all the people around you took all the fun out of the experience, like a vacuum sucking dirt out of the carpet.

Life, like the ocean, is full of different waves. For us to truly enjoy ourselves, sometimes it is necessary to find the right wave. It is only in the appropriate context that we will be able to learn and move forward toward bigger and better waves. In my experience, when people find what they have to do and what they enjoy doing are the same thing, life seems to move smoothly and enjoyable for everyone. The conditions do not have to be perfect, but when we move in concert with the wave it feels great—the moment is just that much more enjoyable. If you don't like big surf, don't try to go out every day in the big surf. If you don't like cold weather, find a sunny place to live. If you don't like your job, find a new job doing what you love. To get there, we must focus on the right attitude and move in the direction right for us, like a vacation to Hawaii instead of Fargo. Don't go to Fargo if you want to surf, go to Hawaii!

Maybe you are like I was. I just did not know what I really wanted to do in life, and all the careers other than mine looked more fun and more profitable. That old saying sums it up, "The grass is always greener on the other side." Or better yet the wave I missed was better than the one I'm going to ride. I find many people live in the past with regret instead of moving forward into the future.

To find the right step forward, sometimes you may need to take a step back and really focus on what you want, why you want it, and how you want to focus on achieving those goals. Let's say you are a schoolteacher, but have always wanted to be a chef. If you can't cook, it's probably time to start learning and focusing on being a chef. Even if you keep your job, your life can start to revolve around your passion instead of teaching. In fact, many people who have a passion for something live a happier life, whether they are making money doing it or not. Their jobs start to become more enjoyable because they have found something in life that feeds their need to learn and grow. Surfing is one of my passions. I love to be in the water, and surfing provides endless possibilities to learn and endless waves to ride.

When establishing your goals, having a niche or passion will help you find what to focus on. I personally revisit this exercise if I find I'm not getting what I want out of life. It is an exercise we can do together to help you find your niche in life.

Exercise 8.0

1. Get a blank piece of paper
2. Draw a line vertically down the middle
3. Get a timer and set it for five minutes
4. When you're ready, start the timer and write down everything you enjoy doing, and that you want to learn more about. Here's the key—you must want to learn more about it. For example, if you like walking, do you want to learn more about walking? If not, don't write it down. If you like surfing, and you want to learn more, and write it down.
5. Ready, set, go!

6. When you are finished, put a "*" beside the top 10 things you like doing in your spare time. If you don't have 10, just choose 1/3 of the items on your list.
7. Now put a "$" beside the items you chose that you want to get paid for doing.
8. Now copy those items with both markings to the other side of the sheet.

What were the top areas on your list? Is this a list that you really enjoy, could learn more about, and feel that you want to make money doing? You may ask, "Why is it important to have a dollar figure?" The purpose is that it is just another avenue of thought to narrow down what people want to do. If you're someone that enjoys their job, but wants to learn more about cooking, don't quit your job to become a chef—just learn more about cooking. But if you are someone that wants to move into a new career, or are just starting your career, then having the "$" may help focus your attention on a different avenue in life. All these exercises are designed to help us focus on enjoyment, on the glory of life and living each wave.

When you have a list of items you enjoy doing—and more importantly, enjoy learning about—you are setting yourself up for a great ride. For the next three days, look back on that list and do the exercise over and over again. The reason I say do it again because your brain starts to think through areas that you really want to learn more about. In the first session, you just may not have thought about it. Like cleaning the wax off your board so that you can surf better, cleaning the cobwebs out of your mind can help you find your true path. Also you may redo this list every couple of months, just to make sure your life is still focused on things you enjoy.

surf for your success

Session 9 – how to dream, setting yourself up for the best ride of your life

"If you can dream you can do it." –Walt Disney

surf for your success

Take a moment and think about the best wave you've ever ridden. Now image yourself surfing an even better wave. Think about how much fun you're having surfing that wonderful wave. You can feel the warmth of the sun, the warmth of the water, and the pure joy of popping up on your board. Imagine the rush of energy and pure glory of a great ride. I bet that was easy—if you're a surfer. If you're not a surfer, do this with something else you love. Maybe imagine the best date in the world, the best basketball game, or the perfect hike in the woods. Whatever it is, just let your imagination run wild. Have fun without any limitations, just dreaming, and feeling the emotions associated with the enjoyment of the dream. Dreaming is a fantastic gift we humans have been endowed with, and it can be a powerful force in our lives.

Sometimes we dream of ridiculous things—especially when we're stressed, tired, or bored. When you're happy, however, I bet your dreams are amazing. What if we could choose only to dream of fun and glorious things? The truth is you have the power to do that all the time!

Each day we're faced with stress and challenges, and there's no arguing the fact that most of us aren't always in a great mood. Sometimes events happen and our emotions respond, or we want or desire something that just seems too farfetched, or something we don't think we deserve. That last part is probably our biggest challenge. We often feel we don't deserve the happiness we dream about. For example, if you're not happy, or you don't have enough money, maybe you feel you just don't deserve it. You force yourself to dream of the wrong things. Maybe you even have a horrible relationship, or one that lacks in passion, and you dream of getting out of the relationship.

Dreams are a powerful force, and direct many of our daily actions. Even if we're not expecting results, we put ourselves in a position to fail or succeed. At the same time, dreams can be powerful drivers for success. Maybe you dream of winning a surf contest, or finding the perfect wave. Maybe you even dream of making more money or living in a new house. Once you allow yourself to dream of things you want, or actions you want to take, if you align your values and actions with that dream, you have a high chance of accomplishing anything. Remember when we set our values in the previous chapter? If you're dreams are also aligned, you start to see the perfect sets coming in and positioning yourself to ride waves all day. Just like surfing, life provides great waves all the time—it's just up to you to position yourself to catch the wave you want. If you want to stop smoking, position yourself for the wave of a smokeless life, and then ride it and have a great time doing so.

Here's the challenge in this chapter—learn to dream. We must learn to dream of happiness, success, and positive results. If you are not naturally good at this, you need to trust in your ability to do so. Often the first 10 days of allowing yourself to dream positively feel odd and unnatural. It might even take longer—sometimes up to 30 days. Here's the key: If we allow ourselves to dream with positive intentions for 30 days, this changes our entire outlook on life. Even if you didn't do anything in pursuit of your goals and values—your perfect wave—if you dream with positive intent, you will be better off than most people. Here is an exercise for the next 30 days:

Exercise 9.0

1. On a blank piece of paper, write down three dreams you have. These could be habits you want to change or things you want to accomplish. Here are a few examples: stop smoking, stop eating cookies, or stop biting your nails. Others could include being happy, making more money, or surfing better.
2. Now that you have your three items, take five minute for each and really dream about what your life would be like if you have already been successful. Just dream and enjoy, without being self-conscious. After all, no one is watching!
3. Do this every day for the next 10 days, and remember to stay positive and continue to expand that dream. If you start to self-doubt, just acknowledge that you have done so, and then start over.

I dare you to DREAM of your perfect life!

We are now on our way to surfing like a professional, except that our waves are the challenges and opportunities we experiences every day. As we start to dream, there is a simple process we can follow that aligns everything perfectly. That simple process is goal setting.

Session 10 – setting your goals to surf

"If you refuse to accept anything but the best you very often get it." –Somerset Maughman

surf for your success

When was your last vacation? Maybe you went to the beach, went camping, visited family, or traveled to some exotic location. I don't know about you, but when I want to go on vacation, the very first thing I do is choose a destination. We discussed this in a previous chapter and now it's time to act upon your future vacation of life. Be ready to choose a destination, or a goal, before you dive into how you are going to accomplish that goal.

As an example: Maybe you have decided to go on vacation to the North Shore of Hawaii to surf the Pipeline. You mark on your calendar when you want to go, and then you begin to plan. Goal setting is very much like going on a vacation. You first really need to think about what you want, and only then begin to figure out how to get there. When you think about a vacation, you probably don't first think about getting in the car and driving to the airport, getting on a plane and then figuring out where you want to go. But for some reason, many of us do this when it concerns setting goals. We get so caught up in how we are going to accomplish our dreams that we completely forget about what we are actually trying to accomplish. This brings us to an important step in your process—allowing yourself to create goals before beginning to ponder the how.

The "how" always comes to those people who are very clear about what they want to achieve in life. The process of reaching goals is extremely rewarding. What often occurs, however, is that people don't feel as if they can write down goals unless they already know how to achieve them. That is the reason we spent time in the last chapter allow ourselves to dream big huge goals before set them. If you haven't figured out how to allow yourself to dream then go back and read the previous chapter. For example, if a person does not know how to secure financial freedom, they may not be willing to write financial freedom down as a goal. In the previous chapter, you gave yourself time to dream. Now it's time to do so again, but to take the process further. You are going to allow yourself to dream—and to set the goals you want to achieve.

People who write their goals down and review them often are more likely to achieve them than people who just think up a goal and then forget it as time passes. Writing down your goals helps you to transform your thoughts into reality. If you're surfing in a tube, you focus on coming out—not looking backward at how you got there. If you focus on the wave crashing down on you, you may just get what you focus on and get caught up in the white water, becoming that unwanted sock that gets tumbled in the ocean's washing machine. Goals help us focus on the outcome, and help us progress through every step in our process. If you want to surf a big wave, focus on surfing big waves and give yourself every opportunity to learn.

Much the same as forward focus, values play a significant part in our ability to enjoy the process of striving after our goals. Goals which are aligned with our values increase the efficacy of our actions and result in a happier and more successful outcome—like having the right sized fins in the right position on your board for the type of wave you want to ride. Goals not aligned with values cause frustration, unhappiness, and a constant feeling of moving against the flow.

Have you ever seen a person win something, but that person was not happy because their heart was not in the game? If that is not how you want to live, here's an important formula:

Goals + Values = Happiness

Goals - Values = Anger/Frustration/Depression

Values - Goals = Anger/Frustration/Depression

As we move into goal setting, remember the above formula. Set a goal, and then ask yourself if that goal is aligned with your values. If that goal is not aligned, ask yourself either, "Do I have the right goal?" or "Do I have the right values?" Values can change, just like goals, and if you have a value not aligned with your goals, then perhaps you need to change your values. Values are only as good as the person who believes in them. To revisit or previous example, if you really want to surf but value being dry, ask yourself if you really value the being dry part. Maybe you value being warm. If that is the case, go buy a thick wetsuit and some booties and go surfing! Consider which is more important—your values or your goal. It is possible to achieve goals which are not aligned with your values, you just might not be happy with the process or the result.

All the previous exercises were important steps toward building a foundation for writing down and achieving your goals. To be a good surfer, it takes practice, attitude, waves, and the right equipment. As you set your goals, do not limit what you think you can achieve, but instead set the goals you want in life and go for them. As you write down your goals, take some time to do it correctly. Do not rush the exercise. It has taken me between a few minutes, and a few days at times to set goals in the past, but the important point is that I take the time—with the result being that I have clarity when it concerns the goals I set out to achieve. There are three major steps in goal setting: finding your goals, aligning your goals, and taking action toward making your goals a reality. If you are ready, let's set your goals now:

Step 1 Finding your goals

1. Set a timer for five minutes
2. On a blank piece of paper write down everything you want. This list can include anything from happiness, to owning a new car, to making $1,000,000, to surfing in Hawaii, to surfing the Gold Coast, to anything. Don't limit yourself, ever.

3. Go! Write until the timer stops.
4. Now find the top three goals you'd like to reach in the next year and put a "*" beside them.

Great work—now you have your top three goals. To be sure these are truly the goals you want to focus on. My recommendation would be to stop reading now and review this list three different times throughout the day. Make sure these goals are something you really want—and want to live with for the next year. You can always change your goals, of course, but focus helps you reach your potential. The three focused goals will align your life and energy to their own achievement. Once you feel you have the right three goals, go to the next step.

Step 2 Aligning your goals

The upcoming exercise has several steps, each of which will elevate your performance toward achievement. It is important that you set aside some time to do this exercise properly. These steps move you close to true alignment. It is just like surfing—you need to go through all the steps to get to the wave you want to surf. That includes finding the wave, driving to the beach, waxing your board, paddling out, waiting, enjoying your surroundings, and finally catching that wave. If you skip a step, you may never find that perfect wave. Invest the time now. Think through your answers, and be specific. The more real you are, the closer you will be to achieving success.

1. **What is the title of your goal?** (Be specific and use less than 15 words. For example: "I want to lose 10 lbs by Nov. 1"; "I want to buy a new black sports car by June 14"; or "I want to learn to be relaxed all the time by March 14."

2. **What is your vision?** (How do you define success for this goal? Imagine that you have already achieved your goal. Envision sitting on a beach with your friends and telling them about your success. How does it feel, look, sound? Be specific.)

3. **What is your purpose for this goal?** (In other words, what is driving you to this goal? For example: If you want to lose weight, are you doing it too look good, feel good, for health reasons, etc.? What are you doing this for?)

4. **What are the key roles others must play for you to succeed at this goal?** (This focuses on people. For example, do you need a mentor? Is your spouse important in this process? Do your buddies need to keep you accountable? Do you feel you need a coach? How are you important in this process?)

5. **What resources do you need?** (Do you need a computer, a new surfboard, a job, different food, better exercise equipment? Write down all the things you think you need—it doesn't matter if you already have them or not.)

6. **What lessons have you learned to help you succeed?** (Write down what you have learned that has helped you become better at achieving. For example, maybe you have realized that you can't afford a new surf board, or that cutting people off is bad, or that you have a degree you want to utilize, or that you want to have a better relationship with your partner.)
7. **Why this is a MUST goal for me?** (There is a difference between something you should do and something you MUST do. For example, if you should eat better but are already in good health, you should instead set a goal that puts you in a position in which you must do it—create leverage for yourself. As another example: If you are surfing, and you have priority, you MUST catch the best wave of the day, otherwise you will look like a serious kook – at least to your friends.)
8. **What values are important in this goal?** (Here's where you write a list of your values which are aligned with this goal. Go back to the values chapter and make sure you have aligned your goals.)
9. **What empowering questions can I ask myself?** (Write out the questions you need to ask yourself to be empowered to achieve your goal.)
10. **What are my daily habits?** (Write down what you need to do every day to take steps toward attaining your goals.

This could include mediation, exercise, making a phone call, smiling more often, etc.)

11. **What do I know that helps me achieve this goal?**
(Write down the skills you may have which could help you achieve this goal. These could include attitude, education, friends, or willingness to complete your goals.)

12. **What do I need to learn to make me successful?**
(Write down what you need to learn to succeed in this process. This could include surfing a shorter board, relaxing, eating healthier foods, or making money online.)

13. **How will I know that I am succeeding?** (Now write down how you know if you are succeeding. This could include losing a couple of pounds, or something as simple as standing up on a surf board.)

14. **What will I do to celebrate success?** (Write down both small and large things you'll do to celebrate when you achieve small steps toward success.)

I realize there are a lot of steps here, but goals are big items you want to achieve, and deserve to have a lot of thought and emotion put into them Always think about the result. Imagine yourself having achieved your goal—will a few minutes spent in deep thought and writing out these steps seem worth it once you have achieved the best ride of your life? During the goal-setting process, imagine a feeling of accomplishment, and work to develop the confidence that you've already achieved your goal. This helps put you in a mental state that is conducive to success.

Writing goals down helps people down their path and creates the fun ride we are looking for when we surf. Starting on a new path makes you feel as if you are at a new beach with a new break. You know you want to surf, but the wave is a bit different, maybe a little more powerful than you are used to surfing. You don't give up, though. You do all of the steps—visualizing, watching other surfers, looking for the rips and other hazards, etc. The only difference between this break and the others you surf is that it's new, so it feels a little intimidating. It is important to listen to this feeling because it's telling your body and mind to watch, learn, and then go into action. This is when you start mastering your goal, and putting into action the daily habits which are so important in achieving your dreams.

Session 11 – mastering the wave

"When the student is ready the teacher will appear."
–Buddish Proverb

surf for your success

Mastering your goals and mastering the waves takes patience, not to mention an intimate understanding of how mastery works. I am not saying your goals can't be achieved quickly because the truth is that goals often can be achieve more quickly than one might think. However, it is important to understand that some goals may take a bit longer depending on what you are trying to achieve. Either way, mastery of your goals takes daily focus and continuous action, both of which align you with your goal. This process includes potentially giving up old habits to create new ones. Moving from one point of focus to another can cause a feeling of loss, but at the same time provide great excitement. All you have to do is focus on the excitement rather than the loss.

When thinking of mastery, envision a great surfer hitting Pipe during a winter swell. Pipeline is a powerful break, and if you don't know what you're doing, a session there may result in serious injury. If you want to get good at surfing that wave, you have to practice. If you look at the professionals that surf the Pipe and the amazing contests that occur there every year, you will see the result of years and years of practice.

Think of practice as a daily ritual you do to achieve your goals. If you set a goal to be happier, maybe your daily practice is to write down in a journal every day 20 items you are really grateful for or happy about. Then write down 10 things that bother you and how you could be grateful for those things. If you are not used to that daily habit, the first two weeks probably will feel weird, like wearing a brand new wetsuit—a little stiff. Feeling uncomfortable means you are probably on the right track. After a couple of weeks, it will start to feel good. Then, after another month or so, the practice will get easier. After another month it may start to get a little boring, but you're still not perfect yet. That final moment is the most important in mastering your goal. Don't give up and turn to something else. Rather, find more ways to make this specific practice exciting. Maybe try a different move, or a different board. Most importantly, don't stop practicing. Keep going until you have mastered that wave and all of its elements.

This last point is important in the evolution of any goal you have. When you first start out, you may not be good at what you are doing. Eventually you become good, but hopefully you will one day progress to a point where you're good at what you are doing without even thinking about it. Now that's mastery. Here's a chart describing this evolution, and some potential emotions you may need to fight through.

Stage	Emotions	How to fight through
Beginner - Beginning a new habit	Failure happens a lot, but you learn rapidly. You may feel uncomfortable.	This is the exciting time to learn, adjust, and continue to grow. This is the stage in which you will experience a lot of accelerated growth.
Accelerator - Achieving some success	Exciting for some, while others may feel very far from their goals.	Each achievement should build upon the last. This is a time to master the basics and build the foundation for achievement.
Plateau - Starting to get good, but not yet a master	There's a good feeling like, you have achieved some part of the goal—but not everything. You may start to get bored or even distracted by other goals.	This is the most important stage to fight through. If there was ever a time when it was worth staying in the fight, this is it. Make yourself push through the fight. Start to teach others and learn from people with better skill sets. Make it exciting.

| Master - Mastering and achieving your goal | You feel satisfied, and wonder if there is more. Set new goals and begin to mentor others. | Once you achieve your goal, celebrate! Ask yourself if you want to continue, or if you want to try something new. If you continue, find a way to give back, and to continuously progress. |

Figure 11.1 Shows the progression of a beginner

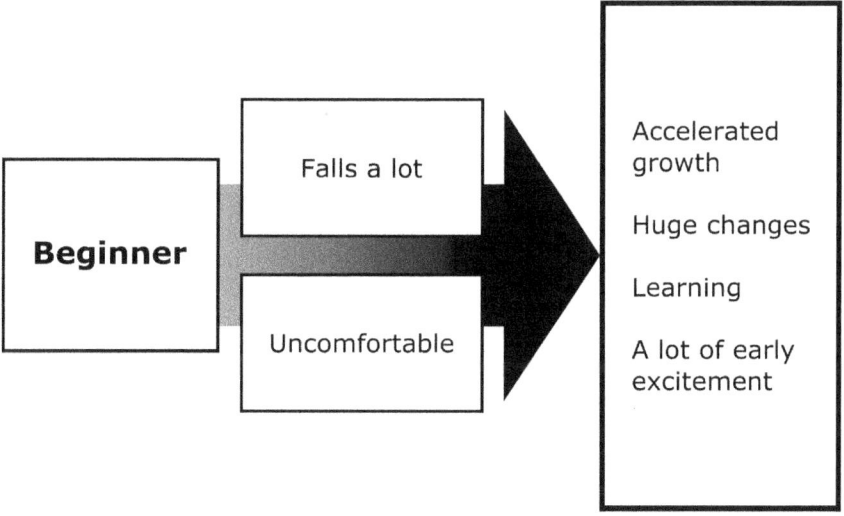

Figure 11.2 Shows the progression of acceleration

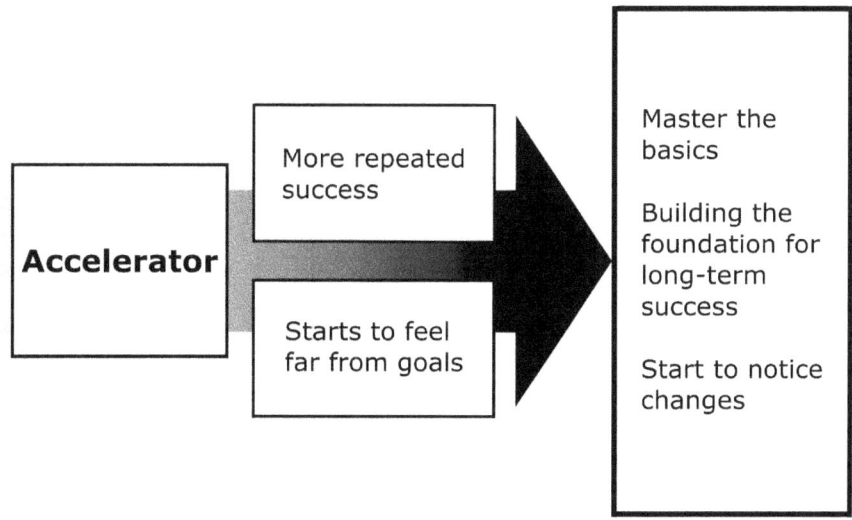

Figure 11.3 Shows the plateau stage where many people get stuck.

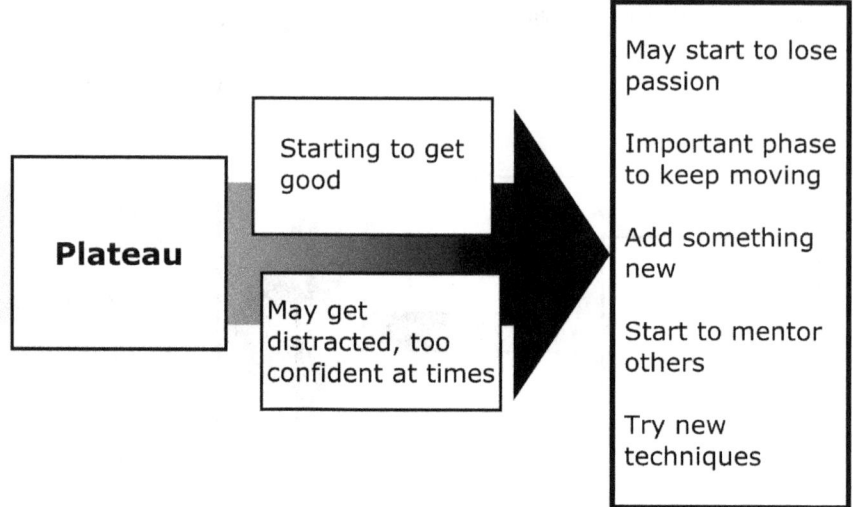

Figure 11.4 Shows the mastery stage.

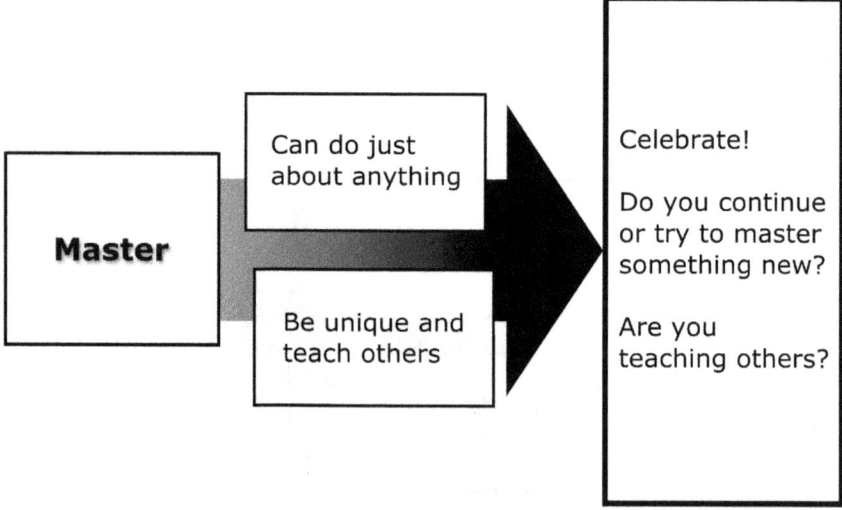

Mastering life's waves happens by overcoming all of the emotions associated with failures and successes. To achieve your entire goal, you must fight through each stage. Be flexible and keep your eye on the goal. It is important to keep working toward your goal, to believe in yourself, and to keep your eye on the outcome. Wipeouts happen—they are a normal part of surfing. When you wipeout, cover your head, wait a few seconds, then swim to the top. Remember, to get off the board at the end of a ride you fall most of the time anyway. It's the ride that matters.

surf for your success

Session 12 – dealing with wipeouts

"The difference between possible and impossible is a person's determination." –Tommy Lasorda

Everyone wipes out—it's the nature of surfing, and often the way you end your ride, falling off your board. As you get better at surfing, you get better at wiping out. What I mean by "getting better at wiping out" is that we become better at overcoming wipeouts. When you take a board, put it on a wave, ride it, and expect to never fall, this puts you in a position in which you will probably be angry a lot. Falling is inevitable—the important thing is to keep going. I remember the first time I surfed. It was in Hawaii, and I was there on vacation. I was just a kid, and the instructor gave me a push on a small, rolling wave off Waikiki beach. I popped up and I was surfing. I remember it was a long ride, and I couldn't turn. There were a lot of beginners taking lessons that day—a true kookfest. As I was riding the wave, I actually ran over another surfer who was in the same situation—we were both heading to shore, totally out of control. Crash! I ran over her board, no one was hurt. Both of us laughed, and then paddled back out to surf again.

Now, if you run over a surfer at just about any other surf spot, you may get a few other words or other things thrown at you, but that shouldn't stop you from surfing. Falling is just another chance to paddle out and ride another wave.

When we have fun, falling isn't that big of deal. When faced with huge challenges, however, sometimes failing can hurt—both physically and emotionally. Similar to the various levels of mastery, falling or failing is based upon the interpretation of the outcome. If you take falling as a chance to ride another wave, it's actually the best way to get off the wave. But if you take failing as an indication that you can't surf, then it hurts. When you start anything, you should expect two things: success and failure. It is important, however, that we start changing our language in regards to failure, and actually consider it a learning opportunity. For now on, let's consider failures to be nothing more than new wave riding opportunities.

When trying to achieve anything in life, we must learn as we go. It's keeping our eye on our goal that helps us maintain enjoyment, focus, and continual learning. We can't expect to be perfect at something we don't know how to do yet and the only way to become better is to learn. Opportunities for learning (which we use to call "failures") are just another way to find out how to get to your goal.

Let's consider a manager at a coffee shop. How do you know your latest coffee creation is selling? It's pretty easy, actually: you sell it, and people comment—"that tastes good." How do you know if it isn't selling? No one buys it. Is either of these a failure? You have learned in both instances, and you can either continue doing what you are doing, or choose to make a change. Instead of getting mad or upset, learn from your experiences and continue down the road to success. It should be a fun and enjoyable experience. Just like falling on a wave—

sometime it's fun and we can laugh at ourselves and sometimes it hurts like hell. It is ok to acknowledge the emotions that come with a big fall. The difference between people who are happy with life and those who are unhappy is the ability to recovery from big, painful falls.

Here are some strategies for overcoming big falls based upon the stage of your goal achievement. Back in the mastering chapter there were four stages of mastery: beginner, accelerator, plateau, and master. Each stage of development also has a stage of failure overcome in a different manner. Remember, don't get mad at the wave—just position yourself differently next time. In the table below I have listed each stage of goal development and a copy of strategies for dealing with either a small or huge fall.

Stage of goal	Small Wipeout	Huge wipeout
Beginner	These happen often. Write down what you learn from all the "falls" you experience each day and ask yourself how you can do better.	Can be a hugely discouraging experience, especially if you experience huge falls a lot. Try to take smaller steps—you could be attempting to ride a bigger wave than you are ready for. If the fall is huge, just review your

		goal sheet and make sure you are excited about what you are attempting to achieve.
Accelerator	Be excited that you are achieving some success. You probably are used to wiping out by now, and can overcome these setbacks. Keep writing down what you learn and how can you position yourself differently.	This could be your first big wipeout. If you have been achieving some success, this could be a good time to spend time gaining confidence at a smaller wave, or doing something you've already done well before going out to the bigger waves. Best strategy: review your motivation, go be successful on a smaller wave, then paddle back out again. It's called regaining your footing.
Plateau	This can be the boring part, so failures can be quite discouraging during this stage. Take	The plateau is probably the most important stage in goal attainment, but it's often the most boring part. When a big fall

	time to get motivated and try pushing yourself harder during this phase. Change up your positioning, or try a new board. But most importantly, take time each day to get motivated. You are almost there!	happens during this stage, many people's first impulse is to give up— but not you. Take time to push yourself through the fall, and try again until you are successful. Find a fresh perspective by changing positions or learning from the fall. Don't get off the board— just try again, and again, and again. This is your time to push through and move on to master status.
Master	Small wipeouts should be easy for you to overcome. The challenge comes if you start wiping out consistently over small, simple things. As a master this can	As a master, you are able to do amazing things and face large challenges— but as a result, the wipeouts can be huge. Take a moment to celebrate the fact that a big wipeout means you are charging at an

> challenge your confidence. The best thing to do is to get re-aligned with what you are achieving and trust you already know how to overcome the challenge. advanced level, and know that only a small number of people could have attempted what you are wiping out at. Now get back on your board and try again.

Take each of these strategy sections and write down your own strategies for overcoming wipeouts for each of your goals. Again, wiping out is a natural part of the learning experience and prepares you for success. The progression will naturally align itself to you when you are mentally ready. You can change your mental state rapidly—some of the other changes takes a bit longer to achieve. Just keep focused on the outcome and be really clear with yourself about what you want. Your body will align itself and achieve your desired success. When success arrives, however, the process is not over. There is still a continuing process of achievement that you must work through for success.

Session 13 – the big wave, achieving success

"You become what you think about."

–Earl Nightingale

surf for your success

I remember the feeling of accomplishment I experience the first time I achieved a major goal in my life. I took a deep breath and realized that after all my hard work, I had completed something fantastic. I would have to say the journey was an important part of the entire process—not just the goal. It was like surfing a fun wave that takes me down the line for a while—a long wave on a beautiful day. To end any journey means you must stop doing something that you have been working toward. But some people undermine themselves before reaching their goals because they find the journey to be so much a part of who they are each day. The journey also provides a feeling of importance. Consider someone that is losing weight, exercising, eating right, and finally reaches their goal. What's next for them?

Once we have achieved our goal, we must accept that change is occurring and prepare to move on to our next goal. There are three phases to this process: celebration, acceptance, and closure.

Completing a goal is something to celebrate! Go out and do something fun for yourself, or just give a good yell. I don't know about you, but after a great ride, I always give a little yell of enjoyment, I may look like a fool, but who cares – it's just pure enjoyment.

The next is acceptance that your journey is ended. Don't hold to the ride longer than you should. Have you ever been out with a friend and listened to the same story of achievement over and over again? This is like the neighbor whose life is mired in the one high school game they won, even though 20 years later they haven't really seemed to accomplish anything else.

The final stage is closure. Accept that the ride is over—you had a great ride, but now it's time to paddle back out and catch another wave. Share the ride with others once you get back to the beach, but make sure you keep catching more waves. The ocean continually delivers more ever day.

As I close out a goal, I think to myself, "What did I really accomplish, and was my accomplishment what I really wanted?" Let's say you had a goal to ride a wave. You trained in preparation and were eventually successful. The wave you rode was on a rainy day in cold water. Once you achieved your goal, you reflected on it and decided that next time ride a big wave, you want to do it while it's sunny, and in warm water. You get what you ask for only when you focus your thoughts and actions upon attaining it.

Every time I ride a wave, I learn something that I want to try the next time I'm riding a wave. I think that is one of the most powerful lessons of surfing: I find that I always want to do better the next ride, whether that means having more fun or trying a new turn. I'm far from being someone who is watched and admired, but I'm always challenging myself to stay up and enjoy the process. As I start to get better, I imagine doing a big turn as I carve up the side of the wave's face. My point here is that each time you achieve your goal, ask yourself if that was what you really wanted, or if you need to set more specific goals in the future.

Learning and refining makes the entire goal-setting process—and life in general—an enjoyable experience, instead of one that ends in failure or a feeling of regret. When I was learning to surf, I got to stand up, but it wasn't until I matured and started to enjoy the entire surfing process that reaching my goals became an enjoyable experience. I used to shoot just for success and I achieve my goals, but that wasn't as fun. Follow the next few steps to refine you goals and take their enjoyment to a new level:

Exercise 13.0

1. Take out a blank piece of paper and write the goal you just achieved at the top of the piece of paper.
2. Write down a list of things you most enjoyed about the process of achieving your goal. (Don't be negative, stay positive – it should be easy for you now to stay positive!)
3. Write down a list of what you want to have changed in the process of achieving your goals.
4. Write down a list of what you would change if you were to pursue this goal again.

5. If you achieved your goal, but it wasn't quite what you were expecting, write down how you would be more specific in this goal.
6. Write down how grateful and thankful you are for having achieved your goal.
7. Write down how you are celebrating your achievement.

The most important part of the process is to be thankful and grateful for your achievement. You did it! You may have just accomplished something you thought wasn't possible, or maybe just took a little step forward. Both ways, now you know you can accomplish anything—and that the process can be enjoyable. Like any great day of surfing, it is about more than just the wave. The wave, like any wave, is just that—a wave. It's how you position yourself that makes the surfing fun. When you are out in the water, you can believe the waves are coming. Just like any success in life, if you want the wave, and position yourself to catch it, you can achieve success. If you want to be happy, just believe, and imagine yourself achieving success. The fun will be in the process. Just like setting a positive mental state and aligning your goals with the wave you want to catch, fueling your body will help you enjoy the process.

Session 14 – fuel to feed your body

"Watch your thoughts, they become words. Watch your words, they become actions. Watch your actions, they become habits. Watch your habits, they become character. Watch your character, it becomes your destiny." –Frank Outlaw

surf for your success

Like any activity in life, having the proper chemistry in your body helps fuel your success. For example, if I go out surfing and I haven't had something to eat; I get cold in the water faster than if I hadn't had something to eat earlier in the day. I'm not talking about a huge breakfast buffet—just something to cut the hunger and provide a little fuel in the morning. Everyone has different diet plans. There are thousands of diets out there, all providing plenty of research to indicate that they are the best diet available. If you don't have a problem, don't worry about it, but what you eat or don't eat also affects your attitude. Below, I will outline the program that has worked best for me but I suggest that you find your own diet and stick to it.

When eating right, people think clearer and are happier—that is a fact. When people are eating the foods their bodies need and focusing themselves on the goals they want, they are happier. When your body is fueled with real food, both your muscles and your brain will work better. Below is a list of good tips to live by, but again, create a plan that works for you. I have tried dozens of diets and eating plans, some outlandish, others very simple, while some have made me feel sluggish and out of alignment, I believe I have finally found the plan that is best for my body.

Think of your body as an ocean. If you put crap in it, the ocean gets polluted and kills the life within. If you keep it clean, life can flourish and balance itself out. Consider the great reefs out in the ocean—well-balanced ecosystems. You have beautiful fish, and predators and the water is clear, life seems to thrive. When reefs get polluted, however, they die off, the water becomes murky, and soon the area becomes a dead zone. The ocean and the reefs are equipped to fend off and process small amounts of pollution; our polluting or over-indulgence chokes out life and overcomes the processes which normally keep the ocean clean. It is the same with your body.

Consider the act of smoking. If you eat right, but smoke, you are still polluting your own internal ocean. In the same way, if you don't smoke, but eat too much sugar, you're effectively doing the same thing. Now, if you have a cupcake once per year at a party, your body should be able to process that small indulgence without any detrimental effects (Naturally this doesn't work if you are allergic reactions toward some foods. If you have allergies or food reactions, it is important that you consult your doctor for a proper dietary plan.). But if you have a cupcake with every meal, you are potentially consuming too much sugar for your body to process. This can cause your natural systems to be thrown out of whack.

You may be wondering how this relates to your goals. What you consume directly affects how you feel, and if you don't feel good on a mental or physical level, you may find it difficult to focus on and achieve whatever it is you are striving toward.

Everyone is different, and everyone's body needs a different diet. Find what works for you, what makes you feel good meets your own personal health needs and goals. Actively make yourself aware of what you are eating, and consider how it will make you feel before you put it in your mouth, not after.

Positive feelings (indicators you are probably eating right):

- Feel light and happy
- Feel full of energy
- You can focus
- You are not second guessing yourself all the time
- You have a core happiness
- You are quick to forgive
- You are relaxed
- You can process events without over-reacting

Negative feelings (indicators you may need to change your diet)

- Feeling scatterbrained, having difficulty focusing on a single task
- Experiencing negative feelings all the time, like a cloud is hanging over your head
- Feeling full, or as if your body isn't processing food efficiently
- Low energy, like you just can't get going

- Getting angry quickly, being bothered by things and reacting negatively
- Feeling bloated

Just like your life values, when your food habits align with your goals you can enjoy the process and the experience. When you have a powerful ecosystem, you can process a little indulgence from time to time because the ecosystem works to process all the good and the bad you put inside yourself. When you overindulge quite often, however, the ecosystem cannot process everything, and essential elements die off. When essential elements in the ocean start to die off, the rest of the ocean environment reacts negatively.

What seems to work well:

- Eating lots of vegetables (yes, eat your green veggies)
- Eating fruits separately
- Limiting yourself to one helping of food—don't go back in the buffet line
- Keeping carbohydrates separate from proteins
- Eating your fruit in the afternoon—this keeps your glucose levels functioning for your brain and gives you a good afternoon pick up
- Eat 4-5 smaller meals
- Count your calories for a day or two. Be aware of what you are eating.
- Stay no to dessert, unless it's a special occasion

- Don't drink your calories
- Focus on foods with nutritional value—no empty calories like high calorie candies
- Drink lots of water, it's good for you.

The last part of any good fueling process involves your attitude toward your body. It took me years to start to like how I looked. Now, I finally like who I am and like how I look. Just by having a positive image of myself, I eat better and find I am healthier all around. This doesn't work for everyone, of course. Maybe you don't like how you look and want to continue to torture yourself by always looking at yourself negatively. But it is important to create a positive foundation. If you want to feel great and look great, tell yourself just that: "I look great and I love my body." Having the right attitude and focus allows each of us to achieve our goals. If you want a great body, have it. Proper eating habits will support and enable you to look better.

Focusing on what you want to achieve allows you to achieve the results you want. When you have the right focus, you will start to surround yourself with the people who support your goals. If you have problems meeting your health goals, look around and see if you are surrounding yourself with the right people.

Session 15 – people in your life

"People will forget what you said, people will forget what you did, but people will never forget how you made them feel." –Maya Angelou

surf for your success

When I really started achieving the results I desired, it became very much about the people I chose to learn from and hang out with. I always had good friends and family, but those people where not always the ones who helped me achieve the results I wanted. My friends and family are very supportive, which is important when we are working to achieve our goals. When the surfing bug took a hold of me, I had friends who surfed, but they were not great surfers and not great teachers. My friends and family were kind enough to offer advice, but actually none of them participated in the activity I was trying to learn. There is nothing more ridiculous than having someone that has never stood on a board tell you how to paddle into a wave. Imagine if you wanted to lose weight—you wouldn't go ask your out-of-shape friend who could stand to lose 50 pounds for advice on how to be thin. Your friend may speak like an expert, but his actions speak louder than words.

Everyone needs good friends. If you want to achieve your goals, find people who can help you achieve the results you want because they have achieved those results themselves. When I wanted to learn to surf, I took lessons from a great surf school right at Seal Beach, CA. I had a great first day with my instructor. A veteran local surfer walking past me told me in a kind way, "Just do exactly what he tells you. Don't even ask questions—just do it. Eventually you'll be a great surfer. He's a great teacher." I took his advice. And I continued to take lessons from him, even though I lived a two-hour flight away. Then, when I moved closer, a two-hour drive was even more worth it. Finding the right person or people to help direct you toward your goals is important, but those people can be difficult to find.

There are two stages to finding the right people. The first stage—and I know this could be a challenge—is letting go of the wrong people in your life. There may be times or certain situations when you have a hard time maintaining your values because of the friend or group you are hanging out with. Maybe you want to stop drinking alcohol, but you hang out with a group that drinks a lot for fun. After honestly assessing yourself, if you find that you do not have enough confidence to say no, perhaps you should consider taking a short break from the party nights—just until you have built some confidence in yourself. I would love to say that everyone has enough power, but I have been in situations in which I hung out with people—even good people—and because of the lack of confidence in myself, I succumbed to pressure, even as an adult. The pressure does not have to be extreme. It can be a small amount of pressure to simply go against your values. In my personal example, it involved eating desserts.

A couple of years ago, I decided to lose a few pounds and really get into shape. We would hang out with our friends on the weekend, and our good friend would make excellent desserts—the kind you would find at a five-star restaurant. These desserts were killer—not just in taste, but in calories too. She would make chocolate cake, amazing peanut butter brownies, you name it. When it comes to desserts, I have a serious weakness. As you can imagine, I would eat well all week, then the weekend would arrive back and I would gain the weight back. I was not making progress. I had good intentions, but I also really valued my friends and did not want to create ill will—and quite frankly, I was weak. Maybe you can relate to this. Sometimes it is the habit and the feeling, not the intention, which breaks down our will to achieve success.

I decided to plan other activities for a few weeks so I could gain control over myself and develop some momentum in my quest to lose a few pounds. I started losing the weight I wanted, and when I got back together with our friend, I made sure to tell her that I was losing a couple of pounds and would need to skip dessert. She was good with that and commented on the progress I had already made. I just needed a break to get aligned and confident.

Now let's return to surfing and catching waves. When you want to catch a wave, you turn your board in the right direction and look back at the wave coming. It depends on the wave and where it is coming from whether you paddle slow or paddle fast. When it comes, you need to have the will power and physical power to paddle at the speed the wave is moving in order to catch it—no matter the size of the wave. There is a lot of activity involved in catching a wave—from paddle to pop up—and it happens quickly.

When you have people in the water with you, you will often get feedback—either positive (encouragement or constructive criticism) or negative (unfriendly razzing). Imagine that before every wave, one of your friends called you names or told you how bad of surfer you were, or even gave you poor advice. Or imagine if some agro surfer was in the water and constantly cutting you off. You might be able to catch a wave or two, and even smile every once in a while, but would you be truly happy? I doubt it and would question your sincerity if you said you love that kind of stuff. I am not saying all your friends have to be rah, rah positive, but sometimes a great friend actually can be the person holding you back. Take this advice to heart: Positioning yourself with friends who are positive and constructive rather than negative and undermining is essential to personal growth. Or tell your other friends to be quiet.

The question is, how do you find a group of people who can help you achieve your dreams? Here are some key ways to associate yourself with different people (Interestingly, when you start aligning yourself with positivity and striving after your goals, you will find that you will naturally attract a different set of people—people who share your values.).

- Join a club with people who have similar goals. If you want to surf, go take lessons.

- Take a class on what you want to learn or achieve.
- Ask someone to coffee and discover what makes them successful. Successful people are often willing to share why they are successful, and everyone likes free coffee and lunch.
- Hang out in places where successful people tend to hang out.
- Go online with Facebook, twitter, or other forums containing the type of people you want to hang out with, learn from and contribute to.
- Be patient.

Finding a group of people with similar interests helps to align your goals, desires, and achievements. I find that when I really want something and am in the right position to catch my wave, everything else falls into place, I naturally surround myself with people who mean something to me.

surf for your success

Session 16 – keep moving, never stop surfing

"Surfing is for life." –Bruce Jenkins

surf for your success

When you are stuck, one of the most important things you can do is to keep surfing. I personally find when I am at a place mentally where I feel I am learning less and less but am still not a master, I begin to question my desire for the goal. When I start questioning why I want a goal, I get out of alignment, and the goal seems to get farther and farther away. When this happens—when everything feels wrong—I don't stop. I keep moving. I keep surfing.

I moved from California up to Seattle for just over five years. When I was up in the northwest, I really missed the sun and surf. Seattle is a great city, and I have great friends and family up in Seattle. But I love the beach, surfing, and hanging with my family and friends on a warm day in December, enjoying the winter swell. After a great winter vacation with my lovely wife down in Huntington Beach, CA, I found I was really frustrated when I got home. I had my business going, and I was working on another business venture. We were in a position where we were not free to move. I was in a quandary. Moving back to the sun was one of my goals, but so was establishing my new business. I was doing all the things I've told you about in this book, but at that moment I was ready to give up and look for a job down in the sun. This went so contrary to what I was focused on that the frustration was almost overbearing.

After defeating the urge to move right away, I re-aligned myself toward what I know was the right answer: keep moving, keep surfing. Honestly, when you're working hard toward achieving your goals, some days can be tough and can get you down. But here's the important thing: **don't stop ever**. If you really want your goal—if you really want to surf every day—**just keep going**. Keep your head up and **keep surfing**. Through all the tough days, through all the hardships, when you really focus and your values are aligned, you will achieve success and be happy in the process.

In life we all go through a lot, but the most important advice I can give you is to follow the lessons in this book and keep surfing toward your goals. I have not always loved my life, but I do now. I have learned to focus on the wonderful things in life, to focus on what I want out of life. If you were to ask me if I'm selfish, I'd say, "Yep. Heck yeah." But my values always say I must do good and help others to achieve my same level of happiness, so it's all good. The first time I stood up on a surfboard, I knew it was all good. Love your life, and surf your wave!

surf for your success

About the Author

I have over 20 years of experience in business, engineering, education, and helping kids and adults reach for their dreams. I have two undergraduate degrees in understanding human behavior and master's studies in both engineering and business administration. I have worked in the desert with kids and have been a senior leader at a couple of fortune 500 companies. I founded and launched a successful company that redefined the way the world consumes and supplies electricity. I have also been a programmer to a CEO. During all of these steps in my career, one passion has never wavered: the true thirst for knowledge about why and how people improve. I have read hundreds of books on self-improvement, management, and the psychology of self-change, and was a trainer for a famous public speaking course. But my greatest successes came while trying to understand my own happiness by chasing my own dreams.

Through all the wonderful things I have experienced, I have still struggled with happiness. Even with success, goals, and a beautiful family are nothing unless you can enjoy the process and the journey of achievement. It is said that the best surfer in the water is the one having the most fun, and the rule holds true in all aspects of life—the richest person in the world is the one having the most fun whether they make a 1 dollar or a 1 million. We see success all around us, but we may not know the internal struggles people encounter daily. I, like most people, have been that person, not really enjoying or being grateful for what I have, not realizing what I could achieve if I simply focused on the right elements in life. Today, however, I am happy and enjoy the entire process. I want to share with you the lessons I learned on my journey toward happiness.

surf for your success

About SilvrStrand

SilvrStrand is a division of a MorningLine Ideas, LLC. It's a company I created to focus solely on expanding on this book to include tutorials, session lists, video libraries, and a bunch of other life accessories. I'm active on Facebook and my blog as I continue to soak up the sun, surf, and other personal development techniques and stories to share. I've been successful in life, love, and business; now I'm sharing those experiences. I enjoy surfing and there is something unique to a surfer that many people could learn from. It's like finding that guru on top of some high mountain in the Himalayas. Well that guru doesn't have to be bald and wearing a robe, although they could be there, but the gurus are also out in the waves living in the moment and enjoy an different type of success. Let's challenge ourselves to live in the moment as we surf toward our goals.

For more information, visit: www.silvrstrand.com.

www.ingramcontent.com/pod-product-compliance
Lightning Source LLC
Chambersburg PA
CBHW061657040426
42446CB00010B/1790